Legal
Highs

Notice to Reader

LEGAL HIGHS

A Concise Encyclopedia of Legal Herbs and Chemicals with Psychoactive Properties

by
Adam Gottlieb

20TH CENTURY ALCHEMIST

Legal Highs
ISBN: 0-914171-46-1
ISBN: 978-091417182-9

Published by Ronin Publishing, Inc.
Post Office Box 22900
Oakland, CA 94609
www.roninpub.com

Cover design: Bonnie Smetts
Cover Photo: Harlan Ang

For information about the 20th Century Alchemist Series
Write to: Twentieth Century Alchemist
            PO Box 170105
            San Francisco, CA 94117

Contents

INTRODUCTION

The materials discussed in this book are legal despite the fact that they have psychotropic properties. Some are far more potent than many controlled substances. They have not been designated as illegal by any state or federal codes, because they are relatively obscure and have never been subjected to abuse. Although chemicals such as mescaline and lysergic acid amide are controlled by Title 21 of the United States Code (1970 edition), their plant sources (except for ergot and peyote) are not so controlled. It is therefore legal to possess San Pedro cactus, morning glory seeds, Hawaiian wood rose, etc., as long as there is no indication that they are intended for other than normal horticultural or ornamental purposes. The materials listed here are legal at the time of this writing. They may be outlawed at any future date. It may be of interest to some readers that the Church of the Tree of Life has declared as its religious sacraments most substances in this book. Because these substances were legal at the time of the Church's inception and incorporation, their use cannot be denied to members through any future legislation without directly violating the Constitution's guarantee of religious freedom.

Those interested should send a stamped self-addressed envelope to the Church of the Tree of Life, 405 Columbus Avenue, San Francisco, California 94133.

Although there exist both state and federal laws against Psilocybe mushrooms and peyote, we have included these in our book of legal highs. We do so because of the glaring weaknesses in the legislation regarding these. Peyote is allowed to members of the Native American Church, because it was in use by the Plains Amerinds as a religious sacrament long before the caucasian immigrants and their progeny devised laws against it. Even today, a number of legitimate cactus nurseries still ship cuttings and seeds of this cactus to all parts of the country with apparent impunity.

Many species of psilocybin-bearing mushroom grow wild throughout most parts of the United States, and can in no way be controlled. Since the original publication of this book, there has been a virtual mushroom revolution. Head shops and mail order houses now sell complete kits for home cultivation of *Psilocybe cubensis* (spores included). The flagrant ignorance of the law-makers is reflected in the fact that in Title 21 the alkaloid *psilocin* is misspelled as *psilocyn*. This small error is a product of the same mentality that classified cocaine as a narcotic in the 1922 Amendment to the Narcotic Drugs Import and Export Act—and deliberately retains the error to this day.

The purpose of this book is to provide the user with concise reference information on various legal psychotropic materials. These include plant materials in their crude herbal form, and chemicals either synthesized or extracted from natural materials. For each item there is a brief description of the material, the method of preparation, dosage and use, analysis of active constituents, effects, contraindications (side effects, dangers, etc.), and names of commercial suppliers. The latter are given as letter codes. The corresponding names and addresses are to be found in the section titled "Suppliers." Because of increasing interest in horticulture of psychotropic plants, sources of seeds and live plants are also given.

Some of the materials discussed are very dangerous and are strongly disrecommended. They are included because many people have already shown an interest in experimenting with them. We feel that it is important to discuss them while clearly indicating their dangers.

Although we feel confident in the accuracy of the information in this guide, we can in no way assume responsibility for the experiences of persons following these data for personal drug use.

This book is intended as a contribution to the world of information and general knowledge. It must not be construed as encouragement or endorsement, by the author or publisher, of the use of any of the materials herein described.

LEGAL HIGHS

Highs

ADRENOCHROME SEMICARBAZONE 3-hydroxy-1-methyl-5,6-indolinedione semicarbazone.
Material: Oxidized epinephrine (adrenaline) with semicarbazide.
Usage: 100 mg is thoroughly dissolved in just enough alcohol, melted fat (butter), or vegetable oil and ingested. Because of its poor solubility in water these must be used to aid absorption.
Effects: Physical stimulation, feeling of well-being, slight reduction of thought processes.
Contraindications: None noted. Acts as a systemic hemostatic preventing capillary bleeding during injury. Adrenochrome causes chemically induced schizophrenia. Its semicarbazone does not.
Supplier: CS.

ALPHA-CHLORALOSE a-D-glucochloralose.
Material: Synthetic chemical prepared by reacting chloral with glucose under heat.
Usage: 350–500 mg orally.
Effects: Euphoriant affecting CNS in a manner similar to PCP (phencyclidine), accompanied with mental changes like those from smoking hashish.

3

Contraindications: Although a central depressant, in some individuals it may cause nervousness. Less toxic than PCP or chloral. Dangerous if taken with even small amounts of alcohol (even beer). May cause convulsions.
Supplier: CS.

ASARONE 1,2,4-trimethoxy-5-propenylbenzene or 2,4,5-trimethoxy-1-benzene.

Material: A chemical related to mescaline and the amphetamines found in the roots of sweet flag (*Acorus calamus*) and *Asarum* spp. It is chemically the precursor of TMA-2 (2,4,5-trimethoxy-*a*-methyl-4,5-methylenedioxyphenylethylamine), a hallucinogen with 18 times the gram potency of mescaline. Asarone is converted to TMA-2 in the body by aminization which takes place shortly after ingestion.
Usage: 45–350 mg orally on empty stomach. Individual sensitivity varies widely.
Effects: Simultaneous stimulant, hallucinogen, and sedative. One or another of these traits may be more pronounced depending upon the dose and the individual. CNS stimulant, antispasmatic.
Contraindications: Should not be taken with MAO inhibitors.
Supplier: CS.

ATROPINE SULFATE

Material: Sulfate of tropane alkaloid found in belladonna, datura and several other solaneceous plants.
Usage: 0.5–5 mg orally.
Effects: Competitive acetylcholine inhibitor at receptor site (postganglionic junction). Does not prevent

acetylcholine liberation. Hallucinogen, similar to scopolamine, but producing more excitement and less stupor. Potentiates other psychotropics, including opium, cannabis, harmala alkaloids, mescaline. **Contraindications:** Highly toxic. Side effects include dryness and soreness of mucous membranes, blurred vision, urinary retention, severe hallucinations, retrograde amnesia lasting several hours to several days. Not recommended without expert supervision. Possible brain damage from large amounts.
Supplier: CR.

BELLADONNA Deadly Nightshade. *Atropa belladonna* L. Family Solanaceae (Potato family).

Material: Leaves and roots of perennial herb found in wooded hills and shaded areas of central and southern Europe, southwest Asia, and Algeria, and naturalized in USA.
Usage: Crushed dried leaves 30–200 mg or root 30–120 mg taken orally or smoked.
Active Constituents: Atropine, scopolamine and other tropanes. Leaves contain 0.3–0.5% total alkaloids, roots 0.4–0.7%.
Effects: Hallucinogen, hypnotic, anticholinergic.
Contraindications: Extremely toxic. Even moderate doses could be fatal. Root contains apoatropine which can be lethal even in small amounts, especially when taken orally. Use not recommended. See atropine and scopolamine.
Supplier: Seeds RCS.

BETEL NUT (*Areca catechu*). Family Palmaceae (Palm family).

Material: The large seed of this Asian palm tree.

Usage: It is wrapped in the leaf of the betel pepper (*Piper chavica betel*) and sprinkled with burnt lime, catechu gum from the Malayan acacia tree (*Acacia catechu*) and nutmeg, cardamom or other spices. This morsel is placed in the mouth and sucked on for several hours.

Active Constituents: Arecoline (methyl-1,2,5,6-tetra-hydro-1-methylnicotinate), a volatile oil, is released from the nut by action of saliva and lime. Betel leaf contains chavicol, allylpyrocathechol, chavibetol and cadinene.

Effects: Arecoline is a central nervous system stimulant. It increases respiration and decreases the work load of the heart. Betel leaf has mild stimulating properties.

Contraindications: Excessive arecoline from immoderate use or from unripe nuts can cause dizziness, vomiting, diarrhea and convulsions. Frequent use stains mouth, gums and teeth deep red (caused by catechu gum). Long-term overuse of betel nut is said to weaken sexual potency.

Supplier: Areca nuts and betel leaves, MGH; young palms, RCS.

BROOM   (*Genista, Cytisus, Spartium* spp.). Family Leguminosae (Bean family).

Material: Blossoms of any of several species including Canary Island broom (*Genista canariensis*), Scotch broom (*Cytisus scoparius*), and Spanish broom (*Spartium junceum*).

Usage: Blossoms are collected, aged in a sealed jar for 10 days, dried, and rolled into cigarettes. Smoke is inhaled and held.

Active Constituents: Cytisine (a toxic pyridine).
Effects: One cigarette produces relaxed feelings for 2 hours. More causes deeper relaxation and longer-lasting effects (4–5 hours). Relaxation is deepest during 2 hours and is followed by mental alertness and increased awareness of color without hallucinations.
Contraindications: Usually no undesirable side effects or hangover. Some persons experience mild headache immediately after smoking. Broom flowers are extremely toxic when ingested. Has heart-stimulating properties like digitalis.
Supplier: Common in parks and gardens. Dried broom, MGH; viable seeds and plants, RCS.

CABEZA DE ANGEL *(Calliandra anomala).*
Family Leguminosae (Bean family).

Material: Resins of shrub with feathery, crimson flowers found in level or mountainous places and near streams in southern Mexico and Guatemala; sometimes cultivated as ornamental in California.
Usage: Formerly used by Aztecs. Incisions made in bark, resins collected after several days, dried, pulverized, mixed with ash and snuffed.
Active Constituents: Unidentified.
Effects: Hypnotic, induces sleep. Also used medicinally for dysentery, swellings, fever and malaria.
Contraindications: None known.
Supplier: Seeds and cuttings, RCS (inquire).

CALAMUS Sweet flag, rat root *(Acorus calamus).*
Family Araceae (Arum family).

Material: Roots of tall, fragrant, sword-leaved plant found in marshes and borders of ponds and streams in Europe, Asia, and North America from Nova Scotia to Minnesota, southward to Florida and Texas.

Usage: Roots are collected in late autumn or spring, washed, voided of root fibres and dried with moderate heat. Root may be chewed or broken up and boiled as a tea. Doses range from 2 to 10 inches of root. Root deteriorates with age. Usually inactive after 1 year. Store closed in cool dry place.

Active Constituents: Asarone and beta-asarone.

Effects: A piece of dried root the thickness of a pencil and about 2″ long provides stimulation and buoyant feelings. A piece 10″ long acts as a mind alterant and hallucinogen. (See asarone.)

Contraindications: The FDA frowns upon the sale and use of calamus and has issued directives to certain herb dealers not to sell it to the public. An FDA directive is simply a polite word for a threat of hassling without a law to back it. At present there are no laws against calamus. Some experiments have indicated that excessive amounts of calamus oil can increase the tumor rate in rats. Many of the Cree Indians of Northern Alberta chew calamus root for oral hygiene and as a stimulating tonic. They apparently suffer no unpleasant side effects. In fact, those who use it seem to be in better general health than those who do not.

Supplier: Dried root, MGH; viable root, RCS, GBR.

CALEA *Calea zacatechichi.* Family Compositae (Sunflower family).

Material: Leaves of a shrub from central Mexico and Costa Rica.

Usage: 1 oz. of crushed dried leaves is steeped in 1 pt. water or extracted into alcohol. Tea is drunk slowly. A cigarette of the leaves may be smoked to increase the effect.

Active Constituents: Alkaloids have not been found in calea. Psychoactive components uncertain but believed to be in aromatic and bitter principle.

Effects: Feelings of repose after 30 minutes with increased awareness of heart and pulse. One oz. clarifies mind and senses. Larger amounts may induce hallucinations.

Contraindications: None known.

Supplier: Must be procured in Mexico. Oaxaca marketplace.

CALIFORNIA POPPY *Eschscholtzia californica.* Family Papaveraceae (Poppy family).

Material: Leaves, flowers and capsules of common wildflower.

Usage: Materials are dried and smoked.

Active Constituents: Opium-related alkaloids: protopine, chelerythrine, sanguinarine, α- and β-homochelidonine, and several glucosides.

Effects: Very mild marijuana-like euphoria from smoking lasting 20–30 minutes. Concentrated extract of plant may be more potent when ingested or smoked.

Contraindications: No apparent side effects. Not habit-forming. Appears to be ineffective when used again within 24 hours.

Supplier: Grows wild (protected by California law; misdemeanor, fine for plucking). Seeds, B, FM, G, NK, RCS.

CATNIP *Nepeta catoria.* Family Labiatae (Mint family).

Material: Leaves.

Usage: Leaves are smoked alone or with tobacco in equal parts. Also, extract is sprayed on tobacco or other smoking material.

Active Constituents: Metatabilacetone, nepatalactone, nepetalic acid.

Effects: Mild marijuana-like euphoria, more intense and longer-lasting with tobacco.

Contraindications: No harmful effects known. Tobacco is harmful and addicting.

Supplier: MGH or pet stores. Extract in aerosol from pet stores. Viable seeds; B, FM, G, NK, RCS.

CHICALOTE Also called Prickly Poppy. *Argemone mexicana.* Family Papaveraceae (Poppy family).

Material: Seeds and golden sap from unripe capsules of prickly-leaved, yellow flowered perennial found in dry fields and roadsides of south-western USA and Mexico.

Usage: Capsule is pierced or opened, sap collected, dried, smoked or ingested like opium.

Active Constituents: Protopine, berberine (morphine-related alkaloids), and several isoquinilines.

Effects: Sedative, analgesic and euphoriant. Mild hallucinogenic effects from seeds.

Contraindications: None known from discreet use. Continued use can aggravate glaucoma and cause edema or dropsy.

Supplier: Viable seeds, RCS.

CHODAT; HSIAO-TS'AO *Polygala sibirica; P. tenuifolia.* Family Polygalaceae (Milkwort family).

Material: Yellow-brown roots with acrid-sweet taste, from plant native to temperate Asia (northern China and Japan).
Usage: 1 tbsp. brewed as tea or powdered and combined with other herbs. Taken daily for several weeks.
Active Constituents: Senegin (7% of dried weight).
Effects: Many medicinal uses. Used in Taoist medicine to improve memory and mental powers.
Contraindications: None known. Too much may induce vomiting.
Supplier: This when available, or related species *P. senega,* MGH.

COLORINES *Erythrina flabelliformis* and other species. Family Leguminosae (Bean family).

Material: Bright red beans of woody shrubs or trees found in southwestern USA, Mexico, and Guatemala.
Usage: ¼–½ seed is chewed and swallowed.
Active Constituents: Undetermined toxic indole and isoquinilines.
Effects: Stupor and hallucinations.
Contraindications: Extremely toxic. Not recommended.
Supplier: Grows wild in flat, dry areas.

DAMIANA *Turnera diffusa.* Family Turneraceae.

Material: Fragrant leaves of shrub found in tropical America, Texas, and California.
Usage: 2 tbsp. leaves simmered in 1 pt. water. Tea is drunk at same time as pipeful of leaves is smoked.

Active Constituents: Undetermined principle in oily fraction of extract.
Effects: Mild aphrodisiac and marijuana-like euphoria lasting 1–1½ hours. Regular, moderate use has tonic effect on sexual organs.
Contraindications: Smoke harsh on lungs, best used in water-pipe. Tea has slightly bitter taste; honey may be added. Some say excessive long-term use may be toxic to liver.
Supplier: MGH.

DILL *Anethum graveolens.* Family Umbelliferae (Carrot family).

Material: Oil from seeds.
Usage: Oil is ingested.
Active Constituents: Dillapiole (non-amine precursor of 2,3-dimethoxy-4,5-methylenedioxyamphetamine [DMMDA-2]).
Effects and Contraindications: See parsley.
Supplier: Spice section of grocery stores; herb dealers, MGH. Viable seeds; B, FM, G, NK, RCS.

DOÑANA *Coryphanta macromeris.* Family Cactaceae (Cactus family).

Material: Small, spiny cactus from northern Mexico and southern Texas.
Usage: Spines are removed and 8–12 fresh or dried cacti are consumed on empty stomach. These may be chewed or crushed and brewed for 1 hour as tea.
Active Constituents: Macromerine (L-α-3,4-dimethoxyphenyl-β-dimethylaminoethanol), a β-phenethylamine 1/5 the gram potency of mescaline.
Effects: Hallucinogen somewhat similar to mescaline.

Contraindications: Should not be taken in large doses with strong MAO inhibitors. Otherwise none known.
Supplier: Cuttings, AHD; seeds, RCS, NMCR.

EPENA   Also called yopo. *Virola calophylla.* Family Myristicaceae (Nutmeg family).

Material: Red resin beneath the bark of tree found in rain forests of Colombia and Brazil.
Usage: Resin scraped or boiled from bark, dried, pulverized, mixed with ashes and snuffed.
Active Constituents: N,N-dimethyltryptamine (DMT), 5-methoxy-N,N-dimethyltryptamine (5-MeO-DMT), bufotenine.
Effects: Powerful instantaneous hallucinogen. Peak effects last about 30 minutes. Color and size changes, dizziness. Aftereffects: buoyant feelings, pleasant stimulation lasting several hours.
Contraindications: Excessive dose may cause headache and confusion during first 5 minutes. May cause nausea on full stomach. Physical pain or discomfort may be amplified during first 10 minutes. MAO inhibitor.
Supplier: No local source of epena. DMT and bufotenine illegal in USA. See 5-MeO-DMT.

5-FLUORO-A-METHYLTRYPTAMINE

Material: Synthetic tryptamine.
Usage: 25 mg is ingested.
Effects: Hallucinogen and stimulant; causes dreamlike state similar to psilocybin, but without drowsiness or lassitude.
Contraindications: MAO inhibitor. (See list of incompatible materials.)

Supplier: CS.

• Other methylated tryptamines with similar psycho-active properties include: 6-fluoro-α-methyltrypta-mine, 7-methyltryptamine, N-methyltryptamine, 5-methyltryptamine. The dosage, effects, and contra-indications are about the same for these as for the above. Some of the non-methylated derivatives are also active. These include 5- and 6-fluorotryptamine and 5- and 6-fluorotryptophan.
Supplier: CS.

FLY AGARIC *Amanita muscaria.* Family Agari-caceae (Agaric family).

Material: Mushroom with red caps and white flakes found in birch or pine forests during rainy season in north temperate zones of eastern and western hemi-spheres.

Usage: Mushrooms are collected and dried in the sun or in oven at 200°. No more than one medium-size mushroom should be taken until individual's tolerance is determined.

Active Constituents: Muscimol; and ibotenic acid, which converts to muscimol upon drying. Some muscarine is also present but because of its difficulty in passing the blood-brain barrier it is believed not to be responsible for psychoactive effects.

Effects: Effects vary with individual, source of mush-room, and dose. The usual pattern is dizziness, twitching and possible nausea after 30 minutes, fol-lowed by numbness of feet and twilight sleep for 2 hours, with colorful visions and intensified awareness of sounds. After this, one may feel buoyant with great energy and strength. Hallucinations and distortion of size are common. Entire experience lasts about 5–6 hours. Muscimol is a hallucinogen which affects the central nervous system. Ibotenic acid causes flushing of the skin and lethargy. Muscarine is a highly toxic hallucinogen.

Contraindications: Before harvesting these or any mushrooms for ingestion one should establish positive identification. Several closely related amanita species are extremely toxic. These include *A. pantherina, A. virosa, A. verna,* and *A. phalloides* (destroying angel). Large amounts of *A. muscaria* can also be fatal. Three mushrooms is the absolute maximum recommended.

Note: Most ingested muscimol is passed unaltered into the urine. Siberian mushroom users make the practice of drinking this urine to recycle the psychoactive materials.

Supplier: Must be gathered from nature.

GI'-I-SA-WA *Lycoperdon marginatum* and *L. mixtecorum.* Family Lycoperdaceae.

Material: Puffball fungus found at high altitudes in temperate forests of Mexico.

Usage: Puffball and/or spores are ingested.

Active Constituents: Unidentified alkaloid.

Effects: Half-sleep state with non-visual hallucinations (voices, echoes, and other sounds).

Contraindications: None known.

Supplier: Some related species grow wild in USA.

GUARANA *Paullinia cupana* HBK. Family Sapindaceae (Soapberry family).

Material: Seeds of woody liana from forests of Brazil.

Usage: Seeds are allowed to mold, are ground, mixed with cassava flour and water to form paste, and dried in cylindrical shapes. For use ½ tsp. is scraped from cylinder, dissolved in 1 cup hot water with honey, and drunk.
Active Constituents: Caffeine 5% (2½ times that of coffee).
Effects: Stimulant.
Contraindications: Long-term excessive use of caffeine may cause nervousness, insomnia, habituation.
Supplier: MGH.

HARMINE   7-methoxy-1-methyl-9H-pyrido (3,4-b) indole.

Material: Indole-based alkaloid found in several plants including *Banisteriopsis caapi* (from which the South American hallucinogenic brew yage is prepared), *Peganum harmala* (Syrian rue), *Zygophyllum fabago*, and *Passiflora incarnata*.
Usage: 25–750 mg harmine (see effects) is ingested on an empty stomach. In its hydrochloride form harmine may be snorted (20–200 mg). Injection dosages are smaller: SC 40–70 mg; IV 10–30 mg. Absorbed poorly through stomach. Small doses (20–200 mg) effective intrabuccally and sublingually.
Effects: Harmine and related alkaloids are serotonin antagonists, hallucinogens, CNS stimulants, and short-term MAO inhibitors (100 × MAO inhibition of improniazid but lasting only several hours). Small doses (25–50 mg) act as mild and therapeutic cerebral stimulant, sometimes producing drowsy or dreamy state for 1–2 hours. Larger doses up to 750 mg may have hallucinogenic effect, the intensity of which

varies widely with the individual. Doses of 25–250 mg taken with LSD or psilocybin alter the quality of the experience of the latter. Telepathic experiences have been reported with this combination.

Contraindications: Harmine is a brief MAO inhibitor. It should not be used with alcohol and certain foods and drugs (see list, p. 61). When snuffed, harmine may be slightly irritating to nasal passages. Large amounts may depress CNS. Since individual sensitivity varies this may occur with 250–750 mg.

Supplier: CS.

• Notes on other harmala alkaloids: Different harmala alkaloids vary in potency. The equivalent of 100 mg harmine is 50 mg harmaline, 35 mg tetrahydraharman, 25 mg harmalol or harmol, 4 mg methoxyharmalan. Harmal alkaloids are synergistic (mutually potentiating) and are therefore most effective when combined in an appropriate balance. Tropines (belladonna alkaloids) also potentiate harmals. Harmol and harmalol (phenols) in overdoses can cause progressive CNS paralysis.

HAWAIIAN WOOD ROSE, BABY *Argyreia nervosa*. Family Convolvulaceae (Bindweed family).

Material: Seeds within round pods of climbing plant found in Asian and Hawaiian forests.

Usage: Seeds are removed from pods, white layer is scraped or singed from seed coat and seeds are ground and consumed or soaked in water, strained and drunk. Dose 4–8 seeds.

Active Constituents: D-lysergic acid amine and related compounds.

Effects: LSD-like experience with extreme lassitude. Nausea may be experienced during first hour or two. Total experience lasts about 6 hours. Tranquil feelings may continue for 12 or more hours afterwards.

Contraindications: Pregnant women or persons with history of liver disorders should not take lysergic acid amides.

Supplier: MGH.

HAWAIIAN WOOD ROSE, LARGE *Merremia tuberosa*. Family Convolvulaceae (Bindweed family).

Material: Large, black seeds within lantern-like pod of Hawaiian vine.

Usage, Effects, and Contraindications: Similar to baby wood rose. Dose 4–8 large seeds.

Supplier: RCS.

HELIOTROPE *Valeriana officinalis*. Family Valerianaceae.

Material: Roots of fairly common garden plant.

Usage: ½ oz. boiled for 5 minutes in 1 pt. water, strained and drunk.

Active Constituents: Chatinine, valerine (alkaloids), valeric (propylacetic) acid.

Effects: Tranquilizer and sedative.

Contraindications: Has unpleasant smell but tolerable taste. May add honey.

Supplier: Herb, MGH; seeds, RCS.

HENBANE *Hyoscyamus niger* L. Family Solanaceae (Potato family).

Material: Various parts of hairy, sticky biennial or

annual found in waste places, roadsides and sandy areas of Europe (sometimes USA).

Usage: Leaves and seeds are smoked in India and Africa for inebriating effect. Brew made by boiling crushed roots.

Active Constituents: Hyoscyamine, scopolamine and other tropanes.

Effects: Hallucinogen and sedative. Hyoscyamine is similar to atropine but more powerful in its effects upon the peripheral nervous system.

Contraindications: Same as thornapple. European sorcerers of middle ages claimed that excessive use can cause permanent insanity.

Supplier: Must find in habitat.

HOPS *Humulus lupulus.* Family Cannabinaceae.

Material: Flaky-textured and pleasantly bitter fruiting parts of perennial vine used as a flavoring in beer brewing.

Usage: May be smoked like marijuana, extracted into alcohol or steeped in water (1 oz./pt.).

Active Constituents: Lupuline (a resinous powder chemically related to THC).

Effects: Sedative. When smoked gives mild marijuana-like high with sedative qualities.

Contraindications: Excessive use over a long period may cause dizziness, mental stupor and mild jaundice symptoms in some individuals.

Note: Several popular books on the cultivation of cannabis have pointed out that hops vines may be grafted to marijuana root stocks. The result is a plant which appears to be a normal hops vine but which contains the active constituents of marijuana. This means that people can raise their own marijuana disguised as hops and not be discovered by law agents. Because of this the government has asked hops growers to refuse to sell hops cuttings to the general public. There are no laws aginst hops but they are now difficult to obtain. Hops are mostly propagated from root cuttings. Viable seeds are rare.

Supplier: Dried hops, MGH; viable seeds, RCS; viable root, WP.

HYDRANGEA *Hydrangea paniculata grandiflora.* Family Saxifragaceae.

Material: Leaves of common garden shrub.

Usage: Leaves are dried and smoked. One cigarette only.

Active Constituents: Hydrangin, saponin and cyanogenic substances.

Effects: Mild marijuana-like high, subtoxic inebriation.

Contraindications: Too much may produce more cyanide than the system can metabolize. Not recommended.

Supplier: Live plants; nurseries, RCS.

INDIAN SNAKEROOT *Rauwolfia serpentina.* Family Aponcynaceae (Dogbane family).

Material: Root of shrub native to India.

Usage: 50–150 mg of root is chewed and ingested.

Active Constituents: Reserpine, rescinnamine, yohimbine, ajmaline, serpentine (indole alkaloids).

Effects: Lowers blood pressure, tranquilizes mind without causing stupor and ataxia. Effects are delayed for several days to several weeks because reserpine

must be converted in the body into secondary substances. Used medicinally to treat insanity and by holy men to produce states of tranquillity conducive to meditation. Effects last for several days.
Contraindications: See reserpine.
Supplier: MGH (inquire). See reserpine and rescinnamine.

INTOXICATING MINT *Lagochilus inebrians.* Family Labiatae (Mint family).

Materials: Leaves of Central Asian shrub.
Usage: Leaves are dried and steeped to make tea.
Active Constituents: Unidentified polyhydric alcohol.
Effects: Tranquilizer, intoxicant, mild hallucinogen.
Contraindications: None known.
Supplier: MGH (inquire first).

IOCHROMA *Iochroma* spp. Family Solanaceae (Potato family).

Material: Leaves of shrub or small tree with tubular flowers (purple, blue, scarlet or white) found in wooded areas of Peru, Chile, and Colombia (especially Andean highlands); also cultivated in gardens in USA.
Usage: Leaves are smoked or made into tea.
Active Constituents: Unidentified (probably tropanes).
Effects: Hallucinogen.
Contraindications: Insufficient data. Caution advised with all tropane-bearing materials.
Supplier: Cuttings, RCS.

JUNIPER *Juniperas macropoda.* Family Cupressaceae (Cypress family).

Material: Leaves and branches of bush or tree found in northwestern Himalayan area. Berries of some juniper species are used in gin.

Usage: Leaves and branches are spread upon embers of fire. Person places blanket over head while inhaling smoke.

Active Constituents: Psychotropic agent uncertain. Nonacosanol, β-D-glucoside of β-sitosterol, sugiol (a diterpene ketone), and several glycosides and aglycones have been isolated.

Effects: Intoxicant, hallucinogen and deliriant. Causes user to move about in agitated, dizzy manner for several minutes, then collapse in hypnotic trance. Experience lasts about 30 minutes during which user may experience visions of communication with supernatural entities.

Contraindications: Not specifically known, but obviously not for frequent use. Probably hepatotoxic.

Supplier: Berries, MGH; plants (some species), RCS, nurseries.

KAVA KAVA *Piper methysticum*. Family Piperaceae (Pepper family).

Material: Root pulp and lower stems of tall perennial shrub from South Pacific islands, Hawaiian Islands, and New Guinea.

Usage: In the islands two methods are used. If dried kava roots are simply made into a tea, the water-soluble components are released and it acts as a mild stimulating tonic. If materials are first chewed, then spit into a bowl and mixed with coconut milk, powerful narcotic resins are released in emulsion. Those who do not wish to pre-chew the root may do either of the following for the same result: (1) 1 oz. pulverized or finely ground kava is mixed with 10 oz. water or coconut milk, 2 tbsp. coconut oil or olive oil, and 1 tbsp. lecithin and blended in an osterizer until liquid takes on milky appearance. Serves 2–4 persons. (2) Extract resins with isopropyl (rubbing) alcohol in heat bath, remove solvents by evaporation. Redissolve in just enough warmed brandy, rum or vodka. Honey may be added to sweeten. A small cordial glass per person should be enough. The first method emulsifies the resins, the second method dissolves them in alcohol. The latter is the more potent method because alcohol swiftly carries resins into the system.

Active Constituents: Kawain, dihydrokawain, methysticin, dihydromethysticin, yangonin, and dihydroyangonin (resinous alpha pyrones).

Effects: Pleasant stimulation after 30 minutes (sooner in alcohol). After another 30 minutes euphoric and lethargic sedative effects are felt but with unimpaired mental alertness. Depresses spinal activity, not cerebral activity. After a time, one may desire sleep. Total experience lasts 2–3 hours. Aftereffects: pleasant, relaxed feelings. No hangover.

Contraindications: Generally nontoxic. If fresh root or alcohol extract is used excessively for several months, it may become habit-forming and cause yellowing, rashes, scaliness or ulcers of skin, diarrhea, emaciation, loss of appetite, reddening and weakening of eyes. These symptoms disappear rapidly when kava intake is stopped or reduced. These conditions do not occur with normal use (once per week in is-

lands). Used normally, kava is stimulating to appetite and generally beneficial.
Supplier: MGH.

KHAT *Catha edulis*. Family Celastraceae (Burning-bush family).

Material: Fresh leaves and stems of shrub or tree found in wooded areas of Ethiopia. Now cultivated in neighboring lands.
Usage: Fresh leaves are chewed or brewed as tea.
Active Constituents: Norpseudoephedrine, vitamin C (which helps to counteract some bad effects of the drug).
Effects: Stimulation, euphoria, mental clarity, followed occasionally by hallucinations terminating in drowsiness, sleep, or depression. Respiratory and pulse rate increase.
Contraindications: Initial use sometimes accompanied by dizziness. lassitude, epigastric pain, decreased cardiovascular capacity. Prolonged use may result in cardiac diseases, appetite loss, reduction in sexual drive, delirium tremens.
Supplier: Cuttings, RCS (inquire).

KOLA NUTS *Cola nitida*. Family Sterculiaceae (Cacao family).

Material: Seeds of African tree.
Usage: Seeds are chewed or ground and boiled in water, 1 tbsp./cup.
Active Constituents: Caffeine 2%, theobromine, ko-lanin (a glucoside).
Effects: Stimulant and economizer of muscular and nervous energies. Aids combustion of fats and carbo-

Scotch Broom
(see Broom)

Coleus
(see Pipiltzintzintli)

Tree Datura

Donana

Morning Glory

Syrian Rue

San Pedro

hydrates, reduces combustion of nitrogen and phosphorous in body.

Contraindications: Long-term excessive use of caffeine may cause nervousness, insomnia, habituation.

Supplier: MGH.

KUTHMITHI *Withania somnifera.* Family Solanaceae (Potato family).

Material: Root-bark of shrub found in open places and disturbed areas of South Africa, tropical Africa and India. Other parts of plant used medicinally as local pain reliever, leaves to rid lice, fruit to make soap.

Usage: Root-bark boiled as infusion.

Active Constituents: Somniferine, withaferin, and other alkaloids.

Effects: Sedative.

Contraindications: No apparent undesirable side effects. Given safely to infants in North Africa.

Supplier: Cuttings, RCS (inquire).

LION'S TAIL *Leonotis leonurus* R. Br. Family Labiatae (Mint family).

Material: Resins from leaves of tall South African perennial shrub found in gardens of warmer parts of U.S.

Usage: Dark green resin is scraped or extracted from leaves and flower parts and added to tobacco or other smoking mixtures. Dried leaves may also be smoked or chewed.

Active Constituents: Unidentified resinous materials (possibly leonurine).

Effects: Euphoric, marijuana-like experience.

Contraindications: Persistent use may lead to habituation (same degree as tobacco).
Supplier: Some Southern California nurseries; RCS (inquire).

LOBELIA *Lobelia inflata.* Family Lobeliaceae.

Material: Leaves, stems and seeds of North American plant sometimes called Indian tobacco.
Usage: May be smoked or steeped – 1 tbsp./pt. water.
Active Constituents: Lobeline—2-[6-(β-hydroxyphenethyl)-1-methyl-2-piperidyl] acetophenone—and related alkaloids.
Effects: When smoked, produces mild marijuanalike euphoria and improves mental clarity. Tea acts simultaneously as a stimulant and relaxant. Lesser amounts tend to act as stimulant; larger amounts as a relaxant. Also, may cause tingling body sensations and altered mental state.
Contraindications: Has acrid taste, causes unpleasant, prickly feelings in mouth and throat. May cause nausea, vomiting, and circulatory disturbances. Smoking may cause brief headache in persons subject to migraine.
Supplier: Herb and herbal seed, MGH; viable seed, RCS.

MADAGASCAR PERIWINKLE *Catharanthus roseus,* formerly *Vinca rosea.* Family Apocynaceae (Dogbane family).

Material: Leaves of everblooming subshrub native to Madagascar, now grown as ornamental throughout USA and found wild in Florida.
Usage: Dried leaves are smoked.

Active Constituents: Indole alkaloids resembling ibogaine: akuammine, catharosine, vindoline, vincristine, vinblastine, vincamine.

Effects: Euphoria and hallucinations. Vincamine improves mental ability in cerebrovascular disorders.

Contraindications: Causes immediate reduction of white corpuscles. Excessive or prolonged use causes itching and burning skin, hair loss, ataxia, and degeneration of muscle tissue. Strongly disrecommended.

Supplier: Plants, nurseries; viable seeds, RCS.

MANDRAKE *Mandragora officinarum L. Family Solanaceae (Potato family).*

Material: Various parts especially parsnip-shaped root of perennial plant found in fields and stony places of southern Europe.

Usage: Brew made from boiling crushed root.

Active Constituents: Scopolamine, hyoscyamine, mandragorine and other tropanes.

Effects: Hallucinations followed by deathlike trance and sleep.

Contraindications: Same as thornapple. Said to cause insanity. Not recommended.

Supplier: Must be obtained in Europe.

MARABA *Kaempferia galanga* L. Family Zingiberaceae (Ginger family).

Material: Rhizome of stemless herb found in New Guinea, India, Malaya and the Moluccas.

Usage: Rhizome chewed and ingested.

Active Constituents: Unidentified substance(s) in volatile oils of rhizome.

Effects: Hallucinogen.
Contraindications: None known. Has long history of medicinal use.
Supplier: MGH (inquire).

MATÉ *Ilex paraguayensis*. Family Aquifoliaceae (Holly family).

Material: Leaves of small evergreen tree found near streams in forests of Brazil, Argentina and Paraguay.
Usage: Leaves steeped in hot water and drunk.
Active Constituents: Caffeine and other purines.
Effects: Stimulant. Not as upsetting to system as coffee or tea.
Contraindications: Long-term excessive use of caffeine may cause nervousness, insomnia, habituation.
Supplier: MGH, health stores.

MESCAL BEANS *Sophora secundiflora*. Family Leguminosae (Bean family).

Material: Red bean of evergreen shrub found in Texas, New Mexico and northern Mexico.
Usage: ¼ bean or less is roasted near a fire until it turns yellow, ground to meal, chewed and swallowed.
Active Constituents: Cytisine (a toxic pyridine).
Effects: Vomiting, intoxication and increased heartbeat, followed by 3 days of drowsiness or sleep.
Contraindications: Extremely toxic. Even just a little too much (½ bean for some) may cause convulsions and death. Was used in ritual by Plains Indians before they had peyote. Now it is no longer used.
Supplier: Grows wild on limestone hills. Viable seeds, RCS.

5-MeO-DMT   5-methoxy-n,n-dimethyltryptamine.

Material: Indole-based alkaloid found in seeds, pods, bark and resins of several South American trees, including *Piptadenia peregrina* and *Virola calophylla,* used in the snuffs yopo, epena and parica.

Usage: 3.5–5 mg are placed on top of parsley flakes in a small-bowl hash pipe and smoked in one inhalation, or broken into fine particles and snuffed.

Effects: Overwhelming psychedelic effects occur almost instantly, softening to a pleasant LSD-like sensation after 2–3 minutes. Changes in perception may occur including brightening of colors and macroscopia (size changes). Total experience lasts 20–30 minutes.

Contraindications: Some persons experience dizziness, disorientation and sensations of pressure during first 2–3 minutes, especially with larger doses. If this occurs it is best to try to relax and flow with the experience because it will quickly pass and give way to more comfortable feelings. One should not take 5-MeO-DMT on a full stomach or when feeling bloated, as pressure and nausea may occur. The drug leaves no hangover or undesirable aftereffects. One usually feels pleasantly stimulated for several hours afterwards. If taken too soon before retiring, it may interfere with sleep. Because of intense initial effects one should never use this substance while driving. Very large doses, sufficient to cause heavy blood rush to the head, may rupture weak apillaries in the brain. Continued to excess this might eventually impair mental functions. MAO inhibitor (see page 61).

Supplier: CS.

MORMON TEA   *Ephedra nevadensis*. Family Gnetaceae.

Material: Above-ground parts of leafless desert shrub found in American Southwest.
Usage: ½ oz./1 pt. water boiled 10 minutes.
Active Constituents: D-norpseudoephedrine. (Note: In contrast to the Asian species *E. equisetina* and *E. sinica*, *E. nevadensis* contains little or no ephedrine.)
Effects: Stimulant. Also relieves congestion and asthma.
Contraindications: No serious side effects known. May depress appetite if used to excess.
Supplier: Dried herb, MGH; viable seed, RCS.

MORNING GLORY   *Ipomoea violacea*. Family Convolvulaceae (Bindweed family).

Material: Seeds and to a lesser extent all other parts of plant except roots. Strongest varieties are: Heavenly Blue, Pearly Gates, Flying Saucers, Wedding Bells, Blue Star, Summer Skies, and Badoh Negro (Mexican variety).
Usage: 5–10 grams of seeds are thoroughly chewed and swallowed or may be thoroughly ground and soaked in ½ cup water for half an hour, strained and drunk.
Active Constituents: D-lysergic acid amide and ergometrine.
Effects: LSD-like experience lasting about 6 hours.
Contraindications: Persons with history of hepatitis or other liver disorders should not take lysergic acid amides. Ergometrine has uterus-stimulating properties and should not be taken by pregnant women. Some suppliers treat morning-glory seeds with poison

to discourage use as a mind alterant, or with methyl mercury to prevent spoilage (symptoms: vomiting, diarrhea). If treated seeds are planted toxins are not transmitted to next generation. Some persons wearing treated seeds as beads on bare skin have developed rash.

Supplier: Untreated seeds, MGH.

NUTMEG *Myristica fragrans.* Framily Myristicaceae (Nutmeg family).

Material: Seed of tropical evergreen tree found in East and West Indies.

Usage: 5–20 grams of whole or ground nutmeg is ingested.

Active Constituents: Methylenedioxy-substituted compounds: myristicin (non-amine precursor of 3-methoxy-4,5-methylenedioxyamphetamine [M-MDA]), elemicin, and safrole (non-amine precursor of 3,4-methylenedioxyamphetamine [MDA]). These and other aromatic fractions combine synergistically to produce psychotropic effect. Terpenes enhance absorption.

Effects: Possible nausea during first 45 minutes, followed in several hours by silly feelings and giggling, and then dryness of mouth and throat, flushing of skin and bloodshot eyes, heavy intoxicated feeling, incoherent speech and impaired motor function. This is followed by tranquil feelings, stupor with inability to sleep, euphoria and twilight state dreams. Total experience lasts about 12 hours, followed by 24 hours of drowsiness and sleep.

Contraindications: May cause temporary constipation and difficulty in urination. Nutmeg oils increase

fat deposits on liver. Safrole is carcinogenic and toxic to liver. Beneficial as spice or in small amounts; not recommended as hallucinogen.
Supplier: Grocery stores; viable seeds, RCS.

OLOLUIQUE *Rivea corymbosa*. Family Convolvulaceae (Bindweed family).

Material: Seeds of vine found in mountains of southern Mexico.
Usage: 15 or more seeds are thoroughly ground and soaked in ½ cup water.
Active Constituents: D-lysergic acid amide, lysergol, and turbicoryn (a crystalline glucoside).
Effects: LSD-like experience lasting about 6 hours, with relaxed feelings afterwards. Nausea may be experienced during first hour. D-lysergic acid amide is a hallucinogen. Turbicoryn stimulates the CNS and has anti-tension properties.
Contraindications: Persons with history of liver disorders should not take lysergic acid amides.
Supplier: Must be procured in Mexico.

PARSLEY *Petroselinum crispum*. Family Umbelliferae (Carrot family).

Material: Oil of seeds.
Usage: Ingested.
Active Constituents: Apiole (non-amine precursor of 2,5-dimethoxy-3,4-methylenedioxyamphetamine [DMMDA]) and another unidentified olefinic substance with an allyl side chain which is the non-amine precursor of 2,3,4,5-tetramethoxyamphetamine (Tetra MA).

Effects: Uncertain (stimulant-hallucinogen?). Useful as stomachic in small doses.

Contraindications: Psychotropically effective doses toxic to liver and harmful to kidneys. Not recommended.

Supplier: Herb dealers, MGH; viable seed, RCS, B, G, NK, FM.

PASSIONFLOWER *Passiflora incarnata*. Family Passifloraceae (Passionflower family).

Material: Leaves and stems of perennial vine native to West Indies and southern USA, now cultivated throughout world.

Usage: May be smoked, steeped as tea (½ oz./1 pt. boiled water) or reduced to crude alkaloidal mix.

Active Constituents: Harmine and related alkaloids. Approximately 1 gm mixed harmal alkaloids per kilo. Also several unidentified alkaloids.

Effects: Smoked, very mild, short-lasting marijuana-like high. Tea, tranquilizer and sedative. Harmala alkaloids are hallucinogens.

Contraindications: Other materials in crude alkaloid reduction may cause nausea. Harmala alkaloids are short-term MAO inhibitors. See list of dangerous combinations, p. 61.

Supplier: Herb, MGH; seed and plants, RCS.

PEMOLINE 2-imino-5-phenyl-4-oxazolidinone.

Material: Hydantoin-group chemical prepared synthetically.

Usage: 20–50 mg orally.

Effect: Mental stimulant with very little CNS stimulation, lasting 6–12 hours.

Contraindications: No serious side effects. Insomnia may occur if sufficient time is not allowed between taking permoline and retiring.
Supplier: CS.

PEMOLINE MAGNESIUM [2-imino-5-phenyl-4-oxazolidinonato(2)-] diaquomagnesium.

Material: A complex from equimolar mixture of pemoline and magnesium hydroxide under study in Abbott Laboratories as an adjunct to learning and memory.
Usage: 50–100 mg taken orally each morning for 10–14 consecutive days. The effects are cumulative. Results are most noticeable when combined with high protein diet, abundant vitamin C and balanced B complex intake, and adequate calcium and magnesium consumption. For more pronounced and immediate effects as a cerebral and CNS stimulant, 200–500 mg of pemoline magnesium may be taken at once.
Effects: Larger dosage acts as a CNS stimulant and psychic stimulant, improving mental faculties, especially memory, for 6–24 hours. Its effects are similar to the amphetamines without causing dryness of mucous membrane tissues and cardiac stress. Smaller consecutive doses act as mild CNS and psychic stimulant and accumulate magnesium in cerebral synapses. Magnesium acts as a catalyst conductor in the synapses of the brain's memory centers. Taken in this manner magnesium pemoline may increase efficiency of memory up to 60% in both young persons and senile older people. After completing the series these effects may last from several weeks to several months, tapering gradually. Effects can be regained by taking booster series when needed. It can be taken either while

learning or while attempting to recall learned material. Assists RNA formation in brain.

Contraindications: Large doses (or even smaller doses if taken too soon before retiring) may interfere with sleep.

Supplier: CS, RX.

PIPILTZINTZINTLI *Salvia divinorum.* Family Labiatae (Mint family).

Material: Leaves of plant found in southern Mexico. Also used for same effect are leaves of *Coleus blumei* and *C. pumila,* common house plants.

Usage: About 70 large fresh leaves are thoroughly chewed and swallowed or crushed and soaked in 1 pt. water for 1 hour, strained and drunk. If osterizer is available leaves may be liquefied in water.

Active Constituents: Uncertain, believed to be an unstable crystalline polyhydric alcohol.

Effects: Similar to psilocybin with colorful visual patterns, but milder and lasting only 2 hours.

Contraindications: Some people experience nausea during first ½ hour; otherwise no unpleasant or harmful side effects known.

Supplier: *S. divinorum* must usually be procured in Mexico. It is extremely rare. The Church of the Tree of Life (405 Columbus Avenue, San Francisco, California 94133) has a large specimen, one of the few existing in the USA. They will send a rooted cutting to anyone who donates $100 or more to the church. Coleus plants may be bought in any nursery; coleus seeds B, FM, G, NK, RCS.

PSILOCYBE MUSHROOMS *Psilocybe mexicana.*
Family Agaricaceae (Agaric family).

Material: Carpophores and mycelia of this mushroom, found in southern Mexico, and of other chemically related species (see below) found in North and South America.

Usage: 4–20 fresh mushrooms are consumed on empty stomach. Number depends upon size, species, time of harvest, and individual's tolerance.

Active Constituents: Psilocybin and psilocin.

Effects: Muscular relaxation and mild visual changes during first 15–30 minutes followed by giddiness, straying of concentration, visual and auditory hallucinations, lassitude, and feelings of disassociation without loss of awareness. Peak 1–1½ hours after ingestion. Total experience approximately 6 hours.

Contraindications: Taken too soon after food may cause nausea. Mazatec Indians claim that constant use of these mushrooms over extended period will accelerate aging process. One death (6-year-old boy) was attributed to the ingestion of a large number of *P. baeocystis,* which contains baeocystin and nor-baeocystin. Normal use by adults does not indicate toxicity.

Supplier: Many species may be found wild throughout USA and Canada. Among them are: *Psilocybe baeocystis, P. caerulescens* (strongest variety), *P. caerulipes, P. cubensis* var. *cyanescens, P. cyanescens, P. pellipes, Conocybe cyanopes, Copelandia cyanescens, Panaeolus foenisecci, P. subbaleatus, Pholiotina cyanopoda.* Do not consume mushrooms gathered wild until positively identified by expert mycologist.

RESCINNAMINE   3,4,5-trimethoxycinnamoyl methyl reserpate.

Material: Indole-based alkaloid in *Rauwolfia serpentina*.

Usage: 0.5–2.5 mg orally.

Effects: Hypotensive, sedative, tranquilizer similar to reserpine.

Contraindications: Similar to reserpine but less severe.

Supplier: CS.

RESERPINE   3,4,5-trimethoxybenzoyl methyl reserpate.

Material: Major active indole-based alkaloid in *Rauwolfia* spp.

Usage: 0.05–2.5 mg orally.

Effects: Hypotensive, sedative, tranquilizer. Depletes serotonin and norepinephrine in brain tissue. Delayed but prolonged effect. See Indian Snakeroot.

Contraindications: Usually safe if not taken in overdoses or excessively. Too much, or in sensitive individuals may cause nasal stuffiness, diarrhea, slowed heartbeat, drowsiness, fatigue. Too frequent use may cause weight gain. MAO inhibitors interfere with serotonin- and norepinephrine-depleting action of reserpine.

Supplier: CS, RX.

SAN PEDRO   *Trichocereus pachanoi*. Family Cactaceae (Cactus family).

Material: Tall branching cactus from Peru and Ecuador.

Usage: A piece 3″ diameter × 3–6″ long is cut, peeled and eaten (do not waste that which clings to the inside of the skin as it is most potent), or instead of peeling, mash ir ot cut it into small pieces and boil in 1 quart water for 2 hours, strain and drink slowly.

Active Constituents: Mescaline (1.2 g/k fresh weight), homoveratrylamine, 3-methoxytyramine.

Effects: Similar to peyote but more tranquil. Takes 1–1½ hours to come on; lasts about 6 hours.

Contraindications: Some people experience nausea from mescaline. It is best to take mescaline, peyote or San Pedro slowly over a period of 45 minutes to avoid chemical shock to the system.

Supplier: Cuttings, AHD, NMCR; seeds, NMCR, RCS.

SASSAFRAS *Sassafras officinale albidum.* Family Lauraceae (Laurel family).

Material: Aromatic root-bark of North American tree.

Usage: Brewed as tea (1 oz./pt. water). Oil fraction extracted in alcohol or distilled. Safrole is not water-soluble. Starting dose 100–200 mg of extracted and dried oil.

Active Constituents: Safrole (non-amine precursor of MDA [3,4-methylenedioxyamphetamine]).

Effects: Tea in large doses acts as stimulant and induces perspiration. Safrole (MDA) stimulant, hallucinogen; aphrodisiac in large doses, euphoriant in small doses.

Contraindications: Safrole is toxic to liver (avoid repeated use). Increases incidence of tumors in laboratory animals. Excessive doses may cause vomiting, shock, aphasia, and death by central paralysis of respiration. Normal use as tea is safe.

Supplier: Fresh root wild, eastern USA, collected in early spring or autumn. Dried root, MGH; young trees, RCS.

SCOPOLAMINE HYDROBROMIDE

Material: Hydrobromide salt of tropane alkaloid found in belladonna, datura, and other solanaceous plants.

Usage: 0.5–5 mg orally on empty stomach.

Effects: CNS depressant, anticholinergic, sedative in small doses (0.3–0.8 mg). Euphoriant, hallucinogen and narcotic in larger doses. Takes effect within 15 minutes; lasts 4–12 hours.

Contraindications: Dry mouth and mucous membranes, blurred vision, difficult swallowing, hot dry skin, headache, restless fatigue. Must not be used by persons with cardiovascular disorders or glaucoma. Excessive use may cause brain decomposition. Not recommended.

Supplier: CS.

SHANSI *Coriaria thymifolia.* Family Coriariaceae.

Material: Purple berries of frond-like shrub found in Andes and of other similar species (*C. japonica, C. muscifolia*).

Usage: Berries are eaten. Active substances also in leaves.

Active Constituents: Cathecholic compounds, sesquiterpenes: coriamyrtine, coriatine, tutine and pseudo-tutine.

Effects: Stimulation, hallucinations and sensations of flight.

Contraindications: Little known about this substance. Some tribes regard it as toxic. Large doses may cause stupor, coma, convulsions.

Supplier: Some nurseries carry related species.

SINICUICHI *Heimia salicifolia.* Family Lythraceae (Loosestrife family).

Material: Leaves of plant found from Mexico to Argentina.

Usage: Plucked leaves are allowed to wilt slightly, are crushed in water (or liquefied in blender), permitted to ferment for 1 day in the sun, and drunk. If fresh material is not available dried herb may be steeped in hot water and allowed to sit in sun for 1 day before drinking. Ten grams dried herb or equivalent of fresh leaves suggested as starting dose.

Active Constituents: Cryogenine (1-carbamyl-2-phenylhydrazine), an alkaloid.

Effects: Pleasant drowsiness, skeletal muscle relaxation, slowing of heartbeat, dilation of coronary vessels, inhibition of acetylcholine, enhancement of epinephrine, slight reduction of blood pressure, cooling of body, mild intoxication and giddiness, darkening of vision, auditory hallucinations (sounds seem distant), and increased memory function.

Contraindications: No hangover or undesirable side effects. Overindulgence causes golden-yellow tinge to vision on following day. Continued immoderate use may eventually hamper memory.

Supplier: Must be procured in Mexico (Oaxaca marketplace).

SO'KSI *Mirabilis multiflora*. Family Nyctaginaceae (Four-o'clock family).

Material: Root of magenta-flowered perennial found at elevations of 2500–5600 ft. on hillsides among rocks and shrubs throughout Arizona, Utah, Colorado and northern Mexico.
Usage: Large root is chewed and juice is swallowed. Used by Hopi medicine men for diagnostic divination.
Active Constituents: Unidentified.
Effects: Hallucinogen.
Contraindications: None known. Root of similar species *M. jalapa* (four-o'clocks) may possess similar activity, but is also powerful emetic.
Supplier: Viable seeds RCS. Plants found wild in SW USA. Caution: *M. multiflora* has 2–5 flowers per calyx; *M. jalapa* has only one. *M. jalapa* seeds, RCS, FM, NK, B, G.

SYRIAN RUE *Peganum harmala*. Family Zygophyllaceae (Caltrop family).

Material: Seeds of woody perennial native to Middle East. (Roots also active but seldom used.)
Usage: 1 oz. seeds are thoroughly chewed and swallowed. Most effective when combined with other psychotropic materials, especially those containing tropanes.
Active Constituents: Harmine, harmaline and harmalol.
Effects and Contraindications: Hallucinogen; see harmine et al.
Supplier: MGH (inquire).

THORN-APPLE *Datura inoxia* Mill. Family Solanaceae (Potato family).

Material: Roots, stems, leaves, flowers or seeds of short annual herb found in dry open places and garbage dumps of Mexico and southwestern USA.

Usage: Stems and leaves smoked to relieve asthma or produce mild intoxication. Roots and seeds for divinatory uses. Root is crushed in water and drunk. Leaves and seeds added to ganga (cannabis) in India for extra effects.

Active Constituents: Scopolamine, atropine, hyoscyamine and other tropanes.

Effects: Hallucinogen and hypnotic.

Contraindications: Excessive amounts toxic. May cause blacking out and severe headaches. Yaqui Indian brujos claim that smoking or ingestion of flowers will cause insanity. See scopolamine and atropine.

Supplier: Seeds, RCS. Other similar species include: *D. fastuosa, D. metel, D. meteloides* (toloachi), *D. stramonium* (jimson weed). See also tree daturas, atropine, scopolamine.

TREE DATURAS *Datura,* subgenus *Brugmansia;* includes *D. candida, D. suaveolens, D. sanguinea, D. arborea, D. aurea, D. dolichocarpa, D. vulcanicola.* Family Solanaceae (Potato family).

Material: Various parts of short tree with drooping, fragrant, trumpet-shaped flowers native to South America found in many gardens throughout USA (especially California).

Usage: Leaves are sometimes smoked. Other parts brewed in hot water. In Andes small amount of seed is pulverized and added to beverages. Infusion given orally or rectally in adolescent ritual among some western Amazon tribes.

Active Constituents: Scopolamine, hyoscyamine, nor-hyoscyamine and other tropanes.

Effects: Leaves similar to *D. inoxia.* Seeds cause mental confusion, delirium followed by fitful sleep with colorful hallucinations.

Contraindications: More toxic than *D. inoxia.* Excessive amounts may cause amnesia.

Supplier: Seeds of *D. arborea, D. candida* and *D. suaveolens,* RCS. See also atropine and scopolamine.

L-TRYPTOPHAN 1-α-aminoindole-3-propionic acid.

Material: Amino acid essential to human nutrition.

Usage: 5–8 grams are ingested on empty stomach.

Effects: Drowsiness, euphoria and mental changes similar to mild (5 mg) dose of psilocybin.

Contraindications: Tendency to fall asleep. Excessive use could cause dietary amino acid imbalance.

Supplier: CS. 500 mg tablets from some health food stores.

WILD FENNEL *Foeniculum vulgare* Mill. Family Umbelliferae (Carrot family).

Material: Oil from seeds of feathery-leafed weed bearing yellow-green umbels with anise fragrance found in waste places of southern Europe and west coast USA.

Usage: 5–20 drops of oil orally.

Active Constituents: Estragole (non-amine precursor of 4-methoxyamphetamine [MA]).

Effects: Epileptic-like convulsions and hallucinations.
Contraindications: Epileptic syndrome is undesirable. Constituents in the oil are toxic to liver and harsh to kidneys. Normal amounts as used in flavoring are apparently safe; hallucinogenic dosages may be disastrous.
Supplier: Grows wild. Seeds, MGH; viable seeds, RCS.

WILD LETTUCE *Lactuca virosa* et al. Family Compositae (Sunflower family).

Material: Extractions from leaves and roots of weed native to Europe.
Usage: Materials are extracted in juicer, dried in sun or low heat and smoked like opium.
Active Constituents: Lactucarium (lettuce opium) contains 2% lactucin plus lactucerol (taraxasterol) and lactucic acid.
Effects: Sedative similar to opium but less pronounced. Formerly used in medicine as opium substitute.
Contraindications: Large quantities may be toxic.
Supplier: Viable seeds, RCS; dried leaves, MGH. Some lettuce opium is also found in other *Lactuca* species including market lettuce, but amounts are usually insignificant.

WORMWOOD *Artemisia absinthium.* Family Compositae (Sunflower family).

Material: Leaves and stems of common herb.
Usage: Bitter essential oil is extracted into alcohol. Sometimes combined with Pernod or anisette to make absinthe.

Active Constituents: Absinthine (a dimeric guaianolide), anabsinthin, and a volatile oil mainly consisting of thujone.

Effects: Narcotic.

Contraindications: Excessive long-term use of liqueur may be habit-forming and debilitating. Ingestion of volatile oil or liqueur may cause GI disturbances, nervousness, stupor and convulsions due to thujone.

Supplier: Dried herb MGH; viable seeds RCS.

YAGE   (Pronounced ya-hee; also called ayahuasca.) *Banisteriopsis caapi.* Family Malpighiaceae.

Material: Lower parts of stem from vine found in Amazon and Orinoco basins of South America.

Usage: Stem is pounded in mortar, usually with other local psychoactive materials (mostly solanaceous plants), boiled in just enough water 2–24 hours, strained, reduced to 1/10 volume. 4 oz. cup is drunk by natives. Others should start with ¼ this amount.

Active Constituents: Harmine, harmaline, harmalol and tetrahydroharmine. Approximately 500 mg total alkaloids per 4 oz. cup prepared as above.

Effects: Trembling within a few minutes followed by perspiration and physical stimulation for 10–15 minutes, then calm with mental clouding, hallucinations, increased color, blue-violet shades, size changes, and improved night vision. Harmala alkaloids are short-term MAO inhibitors.

Contraindications: See harmine et al.

Supplier: MGH (inquire).

YOHIMBE *Corynanthe yohimbe.* Family Rubiaceae (Madder family).

Material: The inner bark of a tropical West African tree.

Usage: 6–10 tsp. of shaved bark boiled 10 minutes in 1 pt. water, strained and sipped slowly. Addition of 500 mg vitamin C per cup makes it take effect more quickly and potently (probably by forming easily assimilated ascorbates of the alkaloids).

Active Constituents: Yohimbine, yohimbiline, ajmaline (indole-type alkaloids).

Effects: First effects after 30 minutes (15 minutes with vitamin C), warm, pleasant spinal shivers, followed by psychic stimulation, heightening of emotional and sexual feelings, mild perceptual changes without hallucinations, sometimes spontaneous erections. Sexual activity is especially pleasurable. Feelings of bodies melting into one another. Total experience lasts 2–4 hours. Aftereffects: pleasant, relaxed feeling with no hangover. See yohimbine.

Contraindications: Tannins and alkaloids make tea somewhat bitter and unpleasant. Addition of honey may help. Slight nausea may be experienced by some individuals during first 30 minutes. Vitamin C lessens this. MAO inhibitor; see dangerous combinations, p. 27. See also yohimbine.

Supplier: MGH.

YOHIMBINE HYDROCHLORIDE

Material: Yohimbine is one of several indole-based alkaloids found in *Corynanthe yohimbe, Rauwolfia serpentina,* and several other plants.

Usage: In hydrochloride form it may be either ingested or snuffed. Dose 15–50 mg (amount size of 1 line of cocaine equals 10 mg).

Effects: Central stimulant, mild hallucinogen, sympathomimetic with both cholinergic and adrenergic blocking properties, serotonin inhibitor, hypotensive (decreases blood pressure), and activator of spinal ganglia affecting erectile tissue of sexual organs (aphrodisiac). Taken orally first effects occur after 15–30 minutes. Snuffed first effects occur within 5 minutes. Initial effects may include subtle psychic and perceptual changes, stimulation similar to cocaine, and warm spinal shivers. Total experience lasts 2–4 hours gradually tapering.

Contraindications: If taken too close to bedtime may cause insomnia. If taken while physically exhausted hypotensive properties may be sharply exaggerated. Should not be used by persons with ailment or injury of kidneys, liver or heart, or inclination towards diabetes or hypoglycemia. MAO inhibitor (see list of dangerous combinations, p. 61). Anxiety may also occur. Sodium amobarbitol or Librium alleviate this. Imipramine may worsen it. Nausea may occur from ingestion of yohimbine, but is not likely when snuffed. Can result in heart palpitations, severe blood pressure drop, and breathing difficulties if taken within 48 hours of having taken any amphetamine, even Dexamyl type diet pill.

Supplier: P, CS.

For the Reader

SUPPLIERS

The companies listed here are straight, legitimate businesses. Their function is to provide herbs, botanicals, or chemicals in general. They do not expect that their products are to be used psychotropically. Type your order, sound normal, do not ask questions about dose, use, effects, etc. If they think that you are using their products as drugs, they will probably refuse to do business with you. If an item is not in their catalog inquire about its availability before ordering it. Include stamped, self-addressed envelope with all queries. Include 50 cents for postage and handling when requesting catalogs.

LETTER CODES USED
IN THIS BOOK

AHD A. Hugh Dial, 7685 Deer Trail, Yucca Valley, Calif.

B W. Atlee Burpee Seed Co.:
6450 Rutland, Riverside, Calif.
18th & Hunting Park Ave., Philadelphia, Pa.
615 N. 2nd, Clinton, Iowa.

CS See Chemical Sources, below.

FM Ferry-Morse Seed Co.:
111 Ferry-Morse Way, Mountain View, Calif.
Stephen Beal Dr., Fulton, Ky.

G Germain's Inc., 4820 E. 50th, Vernon, Calif. 90058.

GBR Gardens of the Blue Ridge, POB 10, Pineola, N.C. 28662.

MGH Magic Garden Herb Co., POB 332, Fairfax, Calif. 94930.

NK Northrop-King Seed Co.:
2850 South Highway 99, Fresno, Calif.
1500 N.E. Jackson, Minneapolis, Minn.

NMCR   New Mexico Cactus Research, POB 787, Belen, N.M.

P   Paracelsus Inc., POB 93, Barrington, N.J. 08007 (Supplies a product called Yocaine. A 100 mg sample and information may be obtained by sending $3 to their address.)

RX   Available through prescription (formerly available through chemical companies).

WP   Wine and the People, POB 2914, Oakland, Calif. 94618.

CHEMICAL SOURCES

In earlier editions of *Legal Highs* we gave the names of several companies which sell various chemicals described in this book. Since that time, government restrictions have tightened. These companies have been ordered not to sell to individuals who are not part of an established research laboratory. Whenever we have published the names of suppliers of chemicals, the governmental authorities have made it a point to contact these companies and emphasize these restrictions. They are apparently not as concerned about herbs, plants and seeds as they are about chemicals.

Most the chemicals mentioned in *Legal Highs* are available from hundreds of chemical companies throughout the United States. To find the ones which carry the substance you seek, look in the annual listing entitled *Chemical Sources USA,* which may be found in any university library, or may be ordered from the publisher, Directories Publications, Inc., Flemington, N.J. This directory lists thousands of chemicals and tells which companies handle each substance. Because of the restrictions, it will be necessary to give the impression that you are a professional researcher who is using these substances on nonhuman subjects. It may be helpful to have a letterhead printed for your research group. Make your inquiries simply, soberly and discreetly. Good luck.

DANGEROUS COMBINATIONS

Unless one is very experienced in pharmacology, it is unwise to experiment with combinations of drugs. Even when using a single drug, thought should be given to all substances, both food and drug, which have been taken recently. Most primitive people fast or at least abstain from certain substances for several days prior to taking a sacrament. Substances most universally avoided are alcohol, coffee, meat, fat and salt. Some drugs potentiate others. For example, atropine will increase the potency of mescaline, harmine, cannabis and opiates. Many of the substances discussed in this book are MAO inhibitors. MAO (monoamine oxidase) is an enzyme produced in the body, which breaks down certain amines and renders them harmless and ineffective. An MAO inhibitor interferes with the protective enzyme and leaves the body vulnerable to these amines. A common substance such as tyramine, which is usually metabolized with little or no pharmacological effect, may become dangerous in the presence of an MAO inhibitor and cause headache, stiff neck, cardiovascular difficulties, and even death. MAO inhibitors may intensify and prolong the effects of other drugs (CNS depressants, narcotic analgesics, anticholinergics, dibenzazepine antidepressants, etc.) by interfering with their metabolism. In the presence of an MAO inhibitor, many substances which are ordinarily nonactive because of their swift metabolism may become potent psychoactive drugs. This phenomenon may create a new series of mind alterants. However, because of the complex and precarious variables involved, it is risky and foolish for anyone to experiment with these possibilities on the nonprofessional level.

The most commonly used MAO inhibitors include hydrazines, such as iproniazid, Marsilid, Marplan, Niamid, Nardil, Catron; also non-hydrazines such as propargylamines, cyclopropylamines, aminopyrazine derivatives, indolealkylamines, and carbolines. MAO-inhibiting materials discussed in this book include yohimbine; various tryptamines, especially 5-MeO-DMT and the α-methyltryptamines; and the various harmala alkaloids. The latter are especially potent inhibitors but, like yohimbine and the tryptamines, are short-lasting in action (30 minutes to several hours). Some of the commercial MAO inhibitors listed above are effective for several days to several weeks.

Among the materials which may be dangerous in combination with MAO inhibitors are sedatives, tranquilizers, antihistamines, narcotics, and alcohol—any of which can cause hypotensive crisis (severe blood pressure drop); and amphetamines (even diet pills), mescaline, asarone, nutmeg (active doses), macromerine, ephedrine; oils of dill, parsley or wild fennel; beer, wine, cocoa, aged cheeses and other tyrosine-containing foods (tyrosine is converted into tyramine by bacteria in the bowel)—any of which can cause hypotensive or hypertensive (severe blood pressure rise) crises.

FREEDOM

We uphold the right of the individual to do with itself what it wishes, when it does not harm or transgress the rights of others.

We believe that it is better to grant people their natural right to use upon themselves any substance they desire while supplying them with factual information on use and misuse, rather than to attempt in vain to curb abuse through legislation.

We are not children, nor are we stupid. As adult human beings we are responsible for ourselves and have the right to make our own decisions.

Those who use the information in this book for personal experimentation are offered the following advice:

1) Begin with doses below those given. If no undesirable side-effects occur, gradual increases of dosage may be tried on separate occasions until desired effect occurs.

2) Do not combine drugs unless you know what you are doing. See section titled "Dangerous Combinations."

3) Allow rest periods of at least one week between experiments.

4) When experimenting be relaxed, well rested, in good health, and momentarily relieved of responsibilities.

5) Do not permit yourself to become dependent upon any of these substances for relaxation, stimulation, etc. Seek your high in health, love, and awareness. Learn techniques of yoga, tai chi, etc., for relaxation. Employ meditation for consciousness expansion.

STAY HIGH — STAY FREE

Ronin Books for Independent Minds